Copyright © 2

ALL RIGHTS RE

licensed one copy for personal use only. No part of this work may be reproduced, redistributed, or used in any form or by any means without prior written permission of the publisher and copyright owner.

Questions regarding permissions or copyrighting may be sent to support@triviumtestprep.com

Trivium Test Prep is not affiliated with or endorsed by any testing organization and does not own or claim ownership of any trademarks of exams or third parties mentioned in this book or title. All test names (and their acronyms) are trademarks of their respective owners. This study guide is for general information and does not claim endorsement by any third party.

Printed in the United States of America.

Congratulations! You are holding in your hands one of the most effective tools for test preparation available. The efficiency of flashcards joined with the convenience and ease of use of a book. We want to offer a quick reminder about how these flashcards are set up and what you can expect.

As you will see if you to pg. 5, there are two "sets" of flashcards.

- The top set has a grey background.
    o The top/grey set is your mathematics flashcards.
- The bottom set has plain white background.
    o This bottom/white set is your verbal flashcard set.

In either case, the question is on the right page and you simply flip the page to see the answer, just like with a traditional flashcard. We highly suggest working through one set at time, so do all the math or if you want you can start with the bottom set and do all the verbal cards first.

About the Math Flash Cards

The Math Flash Cards will quiz you over different mathematical principles you will need for the exam, as well as "mental math" cards. These mental math cards will have simple addition, subtraction, division, etc. The goal is to do them as quickly and accurately as possible. You might wonder why these are included, and the reason is that a majority of points lost on the test are simple mathematical errors, all of which could have been avoided. Students who rely on their calculators often fail to notice that an input error occurred. By working on these cards, your brain will be primed and ready for the exam. You will answer questions faster and you will make fewer mistakes, both of which equates to a higher score! This seems like "basic" stuff, and it is. The catch is most people fail to work on the basics, and that's why they don't score as high as they would have liked.

About the Verbal Flash Cards

For the verbal cards, you'll have questions testing your knowledge of different components of the English language that you must be familiar with as well as the top "MUST-KNOW" vocabulary words for the test. Remember that with the vocabulary words, the goal is not to memorize the exact definition given here. The point is to know the general meaning of the word. If you find there are words you just can't quite remember when you come back to them, try using them in context. Really! Just use them in a couple sentences and that will help lock them in for future recall.

With that, let's get started on the next page. Simply read the question and flip the page to see if you got it right. Remember, work across the entire top (grey) set first, then come back and start the bottom (white) set.

Good luck, and again congratulations on your upcoming fantastic test score!

What are the rules for Positive & Negative numbers (adding/subtracting/multiplication/etc)?

What does "denotation" mean?

(+) + (−) = Subtract the two numbers.
  Solution gets the sign of the larger number.
(−) + (−) = Negative number.
(−) * (−) = Positive number.
(−) * (+) = Negative number.
(−) / (−) = Positive number.
(−) / (+) = Negative number.

Denotations mean the literal or primary meaning of a word as found in the dictionary.

What is Greatest Common Factor (GCF)?

What does "connotation" of a word mean?

The greatest factor that divides two numbers.

Example: The GCF of 24 and 18 is 6. 6 is the largest number, or greatest factor, that can divide both 24 and 18.

Connotations are the implied meaning(s) or emotion which the word makes you think.

Example: "Sure," Pam said excitedly, "I'd just love to join your club; it sounds so exciting!"

Now, read this sentence:

"Sure," Pam said sarcastically, "I'd just love to join your club; it sounds so exciting!"

Even though the two sentences only differ by one word, they have completely different meanings. The difference, of course, lies in the words "excitedly" and "sarcastically."

What is the Order of Operations?

What is a Noun?

PEMDAS –
Parentheses/Exponents/Multiply/Divide/
Add/Subtract

Perform the operations within parentheses first, and then any exponents. After those steps, perform all multiplication and division. (These are done from left to right, as they appear in the problem) Finally, do all required addition and subtraction, also from left to right as they appear in the problem.

Nouns are people, places, or things. They are typically the subject of a sentence. For example, "The hospital was very clean." The noun is "hospital;" it is the "place."

What are Probabilities?

What are Pronouns?

A probability is found by dividing the number of desired outcomes by the number of possible outcomes. (The piece divided by the whole.)

Example: What is the probability of picking a blue marble if 3 of the 15 marbles are blue?
3/15 = 1/5. The probability is 1 in 5 that a blue marble is picked.

Pronouns essentially "replace" nouns. This allows a sentence to not sound repetitive. Take the sentence: "Sam stayed home from school because Sam was not feeling well." The word "Sam" appears twice in the same sentence. Instead, you can use a pronoun and say, "Sam stayed at home because he did not feel well." Sounds much better, right?

What is the calculation for simple interest?

What are the Most Common Pronouns?

Interest * Principle.

Example: If I deposit $500 into an account with an annual rate of 5%, how much will I have after 2 years?
1st year: 500 + (500*.05) = 525.
2nd year: 525 + (525*.05) = 551.25.

Most Common Pronouns:

- I, me, mine, my
- You, your, yours
- He, him, his
- She, her, hers
- It, its
- We, us, our, ours
- They, them, their, theirs

What is Prime Factorization?

What is a Verb?

Expand to prime number factors.
Example: 104 = 2 * 2 * 2 * 13.

Verbs are the "action" of a sentence; verbs "do" things.

They can, however, be quite tricky. Depending on the subject of a sentence, the tense of the word (past, present, future, etc.), and whether or not they are regular or irregular, verbs have many variations.

Example: "He runs to second base." The verb is "runs." This is a "regular verb."

Example: "I am 7 years old." The verb in this case is "am." This is an "irregular verb."

What is Absolute Value?

What are Adjectives?

The absolute value of a number is its distance from zero, not its value.

So in $|x| = a$, "x" will equal "-a" as well as "a." Likewise, $|3| = 3$, and $|-3| = 3$.

Equations with absolute values will have two answers. Solve each absolute value possibility separately. All solutions must be checked into the original equation.

Adjectives are words that describe a noun and give more information. Take the sentence: "The boy hit the ball." If you want to know more about the noun "boy," then you could use an adjective to describe it. "The little boy hit the ball." An adjective simply provides more information about a noun or subject in a sentence.

Describe Mean, Median, and Mode?

What is an Adverb?

Mean is a math term for "average." Total all terms and divide by the number of terms.

Median is the middle number of a given set, found after the numbers have all been put in numerical order. In the case of a set of even numbers, the middle two numbers are averaged.

Mode is the number which occurs most frequently within a given set.

Adverbs are similar to adjectives in that they provide more information; however, they describe verbs, adjectives, and even other adverbs. They do not describe nouns – that's an adjective's job.

Take the sentence: "The doctor said she hired a new employee."

It would give more information to say: "The doctor said she recently hired a new employee." Now we know more about how the action was executed. Adverbs typically describe when or how something has happened, how it looks, how it feels, etc.

What is an Arithmetic Sequence?

What is a Root?

Each term is equal to the previous term plus x.

Example: 2, 5, 8, 11.
2 + 3 = 5; 5 + 3 = 8 ... etc.
x = 3.

Roots are the building blocks of all words. Every word is either a root itself or has a root. Just as a plant cannot grow without roots, neither can vocabulary, because a word must have a root to give it meaning.

Example: The test instructions were *unclear*.

The root is what is left when you strip away all the prefixes and suffixes from a word. In this case, take away the prefix "un-," and you have the root clear.

What is a Geometric Sequence?

What are Prefixes?

Each term is equal to the previous term multiplied by x.

Example: 2, 4, 8, 16.
    x = 2.

Prefixes are syllables added to the beginning of a word and suffixes are syllables added to the end of the word. Both carry assigned meanings. The common name for prefixes and suffixes is affixes.

Let's use the word *prefix* itself as an example:

Fix means to place something securely.
Pre means before.
Prefix means to place something before or in front.

What is the formula for Percent? Part? Whole?

What are Suffixes?

Part = Percent * Whole.
Percent = Part / Whole.
Whole = Part / Percent.

Example: Jim spent 30% of his paycheck at the fair. He spent $15 for a hat, $30 for a shirt, and $20 playing games. How much was his check? (Round to nearest dollar.)

Whole = 65 / .30 = $217.00.

Suffixes come after the root of a word.

> Example: Feminism

> Femin is a root. It means female, woman.

> -ism means act, practice or process.

> Feminism is the defining and establishing of equal political, economic, and social rights for women.

What are the formulas for Percent Change, Increase, and Decrease?

"The medication must be properly administered to the patient."

Which of the words in the above sentence is an adverb?
- a. Medication.
- b. Properly.
- c. Administered.
- d. Patient.

Percent Change = Amount of Change / Original Amount * 100.

Percent Increase = (New Amount − Original Amount) / Original Amount * 100.

Percent Decrease = (Original Amount − New Amount) / Original Amount * 100.

Amount Increase (or Decrease) = Original Price * Percent Markup (or Markdown).

Original Price = New Price / (Whole - Percent Markdown [or Markup]).

Answer: b)

"Properly" is the adverb which describes the verb "administered."

What are the formulas for Repeated Percent Change?

"The old man had trouble walking if he did not have his walker and had a long way to go."

What is the subject of the sentence?
        a. Walker.
        b. His.
        c. Trouble.
        d. Man.

Increase: Final amount = Original Amount * (1 + rate) # of changes.

Decrease: Final Amount = Original Amount * (1 − rate) # of changes.

Example: The weight of a tube of toothpaste decreases by 3% each time it is used. If it weighed 76.5 grams when new, what is its weight in grams after 15 uses?

Final amount = 76.5 * (1 - .3)15.
76.5 * (.97)15 = 48.44 grams.

Answer: d)
Although there are other nouns in the sentence, the "man" is the subject.

What is Combined Average?

"The boy decided ___ would ride his bike now that the sun was shining."

Which of the following pronouns completes the sentence?
    a. His.
    b. Him.
    c. He.
    d. They.

Weigh each average individual average before determining the sum.

Example: If Cory averaged 3 hits per game during the summer and 2 hits per game during the fall and played 7 games in the summer and 8 games in the fall, what was his hit average overall?

>Summer: 3 * 7 = 21.
>Fall: 2 * 8 = 16.
>Sum: 21 + 16 = 37.
>
>Total number of games: 7 + 8 = 15.
>Calculate average: 37/15 = ~ 2.47

hits/game.

Answer: c)
"He" is the correct answer; the other pronouns are possessive or otherwise in the wrong tense.

How do you solve Ratios?

"The impatient student hurried through the test and failed as a result."

Which word is an adjective?
    a. Hurried.
    b. Result.
    c. Impatient.
    d. Student.

To solve a ratio, simply find the equivalent fraction. To distribute a whole across a ratio:

Total all parts.
Divide the whole by the total number of parts.
Multiply quotient by corresponding part of ratio.

Example: There are 90 voters in a room, and they are either Democrat or Republican. The ratio of Democrats to Republicans is 5:4. How many Republicans are there?

        5 + 4 = 9.
        90 / 9 = 10.
        10 * 4 = 40 Republicans.

Answer: c)
"Impatient" describes the noun "student."

What are Direct Proportions?

Correct the verb: "The nurse decided it were a good time to follow up with a patient about their medication."
    a. Was.
    b. Is.
    c. Has.
    d. No error.

Corresponding ratio parts change in the same direction (increase/decrease).

Answer: a)
"Was" is the correct answer; the other choices are in the wrong tense.

What are Indirect Proportions?

To take precaution is to:
 a. Prepare before doing something.
 b. Remember something that happened earlier.
 c. Become aware of something for the first time.
 d. Try to do something again.

Corresponding ratio parts change in opposite directions (as one part increases the other decreases).

Example: A train traveling 120 miles takes 3 hours to get to its destination. How long will it take if the train travels 180 miles?

120 mph: 180 mph is to x hours: 3 hours. (Write as fraction and cross multiply.)
　　　　120/3 = 180/x.
　　　　540 = 120x.
　　　　x = 4.5 hours.

Answer: a) Prepare before doing something.
Pre- means before; to take caution is to be careful or take heed.

What is the formula for the Root of a Product?

To reorder a list is to:
        a. Use the same order again.
        b. Put the list in a new order.
        c. Get rid of the list.
        d. Find the list.

$$\sqrt[n]{a \cdot b} = \sqrt[n]{a} \cdot \sqrt[n]{b}.$$

Answer: b) Put the list in a new order.
Re- means again. In this case, order means organize. Reorder then means to organize the list again or to put the list into a different order.

What is the formula for the Root of a Quotient?

An antidote to a disease is:
  a. Something that is part of the disease.
  b. Something that works against the disease.
  c. Something that makes the disease worse.
  d. Something that has nothing to do with the disease.

$$\sqrt[n]{\frac{a}{b}} = \frac{\sqrt[n]{a}}{\sqrt[n]{b}}.$$

Answer: b) Something that works against the disease.
The prefix anti- means against. An antidote is something that works against a disease or a poison.

What is the formula for Fractional Exponents?

Someone who is multiethnic:
    a. Likes only certain kinds of people.
    b. Lives in the land of his or her birth.
    c. Is from a different country.
    d. Has many different ethnicities.

$$\sqrt[n]{a^m} = a^{m/n}$$

Answer: d) Has many different ethnicities.

The prefix multi- means many. Someone who is multiethnic has relatives from many different ethnic groups.

What is formula for the Fundamental Counting Principle?

Someone who is misinformed has been:
 a. Taught something new.
 b. Told the truth.
 c. Forgotten.
 d. Given incorrect information.

(The number of possibilities of an event happening) * (the number of possibilities of another event happening) = the total number of possibilities.

Example: If you take a multiple choice test with 5 questions, with 4 answer choices for each question, how many test result possibilities are there?

Solution: Question 1 has 4 choices; question 2 has 4 choices; etc.
4 *4 * 4 * 4 * 4 (one for each question) = 1024 possible test results.

Answer: d) Given incorrect information.

Mis- means opposite, and to be informed is to have the correct information.

What are Literal Equations?

Define abate:

Equations with more than one variable. Solve in terms of one variable first.

Example: Solve for y: $4x + 3y = 3x + 2y$.

    Combine like terms: $3y - 2y = 4x - 2x$.

    Solve for y: $y = 2x$.

become less in amount or intensity

What are Linear Systems?

Define abdicate:

A linear system requires the solving of two literal equations simultaneously. There are two different methods (Substitution and Addition) that can be used to solve linear systems.

to give up or leave

What are Linear Equations?

Define aberration:

An equation for a straight line. The variable CANNOT have an exponent, square roots, cube roots, etc.

Example: $y = 2x + 1$ is a straight line, with "1" being the y-intercept, and "2" being the positive slope.

a state or condition very different from the norm

What are Inequalities? How are they solved?

Define abbreviate:

Inequalities are solved like linear and algebraic equations, except the sign must be reversed when dividing by a negative number.

Example: $-7x + 2 < 6 - 5x$.

Step 1 – Combine like terms: $-2x < 4$.
Step 2 – Solve for x. (Reverse the sign): $x > -2$.

to shorten or abridge

What are the rules for exponents?

Define abstain:

Rule	Example
$x^0 = 1$	$5^0 = 1$
$x^1 = x$	$5^1 = 5$
$x^a \cdot x^b = x^{a+b}$	$5^2 * 5^3 = 5^5$
$(xy)^a = x^a y^a$	$(5*6)^2 = 5^2 * 6^2 = 25 * 36$
$(x^a)^b = x^{ab}$	$(5^2)^3 = 5^6$
$(x/y)^a = x^a/y^a$	$(10/5)^2 = 10^2/5^2 = 100/25$
$x^a/y^b = x^{a-b}$	$5^4/5^3 = 5^1 = 5$ (remember $x \neq 0$)
$x^{1/a} = \sqrt[a]{x}$	$25^{1/2} = \sqrt[2]{25} = 5$
$x^{-a} = \dfrac{1}{x^a}$	$5^{-2} = \dfrac{1}{5^2} = \dfrac{1}{25}$ (remember $x \neq 0$)

choose to avoid or not participate

What are Permutations?

Define adversity:

The number of ways a set number of items can be arranged. Recognized by the use of a factorial (n!), with n being the number of items.

If n = 3, then 3! = 3 * 2 * 1 = 6. If you need to arrange n number of things but x number are alike, then n! is divided by x!

Example: How many different ways can the letters in the word balance be arranged?

Solution: There are 7 letters, so n! = 7! But 2 letters are the same, so x! = 2! Set up the equation:
(7* 6* 5* 4* 3* 2* 1)/(2* 1) = 2540 ways.

a state of burden or hardship

How do you calculate the number of possible combinations?

Define adulation:

To calculate total number of possible combinations, use the formula: n!/r! (n-r)!
Where n = # of objects; and r = # of objects selected at a time.

Example: If seven people are selected in groups of three, how many different combinations are possible?

Solution:
(7* 6* 5* 4* 3* 2* 1)/((3*2* 1)(7-3)) = 210 possible combinations.

Excessive praise and flattery

How do you factor Quadratics?

Define aesthetic:

Factoring: converting $ax^2 + bx + c$ to factored form. Find two numbers that are factors of c and whose sum is b.
Example: Factor $2x^2 + 12x + 18 = 0$.

Factor out a common monomial: $2(x^2 - 6x + 9)$.
Find two factors of 9 and sum to -6: $2(x - \_)(x - \_)$.
Fill in the binomials: $2(x - 3)(x - 3)$.

To solve, set each to = 0: $x - 3 = 0; x = 3$.

If the equation cannot be factored (there are no two factors of c that sum to = b), the quadratic formula is used. $x = (-b \pm \sqrt{b^2 - 4ac})/2a$

concerning or an appreciation of beauty, art, or design

What is an Acute Angle?

Define amicable:

Angle that measures less than 90°.

characterized by friendship and good will

What is an Acute Triangle?

Define amenable:

Each angle measures less than 90°.

open to suggestion and willing to follow advice

What is an Obtuse Angle?

Define antiquated:

Measures greater than 90 °.

obsolete, old, out of fashion

What is an Obtuse Triangle?

Define anachronistic:

One angle measures greater than 90°.

out of date or belonging to another time

What are Adjacent Angles?

Define anecdote:

Angles sharing a side and a vertex.

a short story or account of an event

What are Complementary Angles?

Define antagonist:

Adjacent angles that sum to 90°.

An opponent; someone in conflict with the hero of a story

What are Supplementary Angles?

Define arid:

Adjacent angles that sum to 180°.

lacking water or rainfall

What are Vertical Angles?

Define asylum:

Angles that are opposite of each other. They are always congruent (equal in measure).

shelter from danger or hardship

What is an Equilateral Triangle?

Define assiduous:

All angles of the triangle are equal.

Very careful and hardworking

What is an Isosceles Triangle?

Define benevolent:

Two sides and two angles are equal.

showing sympathy, understanding, and generosity

What does Scalene mean?

Define bias:

No equal angles.

an unfair preference of dislike of something

What are Parallel Lines?

Define boisterous:

Lines that will never intersect. Y ll X means line Y is parallel to line X.

Rough, rowdy, and unruly

Describe Perpendicular lines?

Define brazen:

Lines that intersect or cross to form 90° angles.

Bold or unrestrained by normal standards

What is a Transversal Line?

Define brusque:

A line that crosses parallel lines.

attitude of shortness, rudeness; gruff

What is a Bisector?

Define camaraderie:

Any line that cuts a line segment, angle, or polygon exactly in half.

the quality of familiarity or friendship

What is a Polygon?

Define capacious:

Any enclosed plane shape with three or more connecting sides (ex. a triangle).

large in size or capacity

What is a Regular Polygon?

Define censure:

Has all equal sides and equal angles (ex. square).

Disapproval or several criticize

What is an Arc?

Define circuitous:

A portion of a circle's edge.

lengthy due to being indirect or roundabout

What is a Chord?

Define clairvoyant:

A line segment that connects two different points on a circle.

a person with the ability to read minds or see the future

What is a Tangent?

Define clandestine:

Something that touches a circle at only one point without crossing through it.

secret and concealed

What is the formula for the Sum of Angles?

Define collaborate:

The sum of angles of a polygon can be calculated using: $(n-1)180°$
when n = the number of sides.

work together on a common project

What are Trapezoids?

Define collateral:

Four-sided polygon, in which the bases (and only the bases) are parallel.

adjoining or accompanying

What is an Isosceles Trapezoid?

Define compassion:

Base angles are congruent.

awareness and sympathy for the suffering of others

What is a Rhombus?

Define compromise:

Four-sided polygon, in which all four sides are congruent and opposite sides are parallel.

an accommodation in which both sides make concessions

What are the formulas for the Area and Perimeter of a Rhombus?

Define condescending:

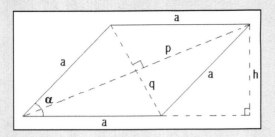

$Perimeter = 4a$

$Area = a^2 \sin \alpha = a * h = \dfrac{1}{2}pq$

$4a^2 = p^2 + q^2$

an attitude of superiority or being snobby towards others

What are the formulas for the Area and Perimeter of a Rectangle?

Define conditional:

$d = \sqrt{a^2 + h^2}$

$a = \sqrt{d^2 - h^2}$

$h = \sqrt{d^2 - a^2}$

$Perimeter = 2a + 2h$

$Area = a \cdot h$

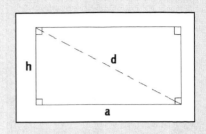

dependent on something else being done

What are the formulas for the Area and Perimeter of a Square?

Define conformist:

$d = a\sqrt{2}$

$Perimeter = 4a = 2d\sqrt{2}$

$Area = a^2 = \dfrac{1}{2}d^2$

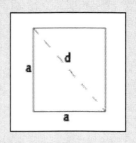

someone who follows standards or rules of conduct

What are the formulas for the Area of a Circle?

Define congregation:

$d = 2r$

$Perimeter = 2\pi r = \pi d$

$Area = \pi r^2$

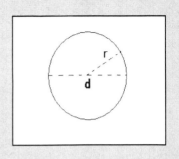

a gathering or crowd of people

What are the formulas for the Area and Volume of a Cube?

Define convergence:

$r = a\sqrt{2}$

$d = a\sqrt{3}$

$Area = 6a^2$

$Volume = a^3$

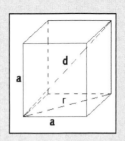

the act of coming together; joining of parts

What are the formulas for the Area and Volume of a Cuboid?

Define cursory:

$$d = \sqrt{a^2 + b^2 + c^2}$$
$$A = 2(ab + ac + bc)$$
$$V = abc$$

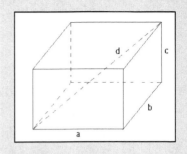

quickly and superficially done

What are the formulas for the Area and Volume of a Pyramid?

Define copious:

$$A_{lateral} = a\sqrt{h^2 + \left(\frac{b}{2}\right)^2} + b\sqrt{h^2 + \left(\frac{a}{2}\right)^2}$$

$d = \sqrt{a^2 + b^2}$

$A_{base} = ab$

$A_{total} = A_{lateral} + A_{base}$

$V = \dfrac{1}{3}abh$

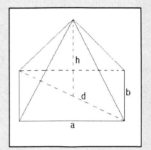

abundant and plentiful

What are the formulas for the Area and Volume of a Cylinder?

Define concise:

$d = 2r$

$A_{surface} = 2\pi rh$

$A_{base} = 2\pi r^2$

$Area = A_{surface} + A_{base}$

$ = 2\pi r(h + r)$

$Volume = \pi r^2 h$

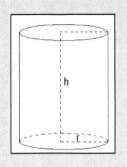

brief, condensed

What are the formulas for the Areas and Volume of a Cone?

Define deleterious:

$d = 2r$

$A_{surface} = \pi r s$

$A_{base} = \pi r^2$

$Area = A_{surface} + A_{base}$

$ = 2\pi r (h + r)$

$Volume = \dfrac{1}{3} \pi r^2 h$

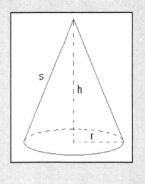

harmful or deadly to living things

Sine equation?

Define surreptitious:

Opposite/Hypotenuse (SOH)

staying concealed and trying to avoid being noticed

Cosine equation?

Define tactful:

Adjacent/Hypotenuse (CAH)

showing concern to not offend others

Tangent equation?

Define tenacious:

Opposite/Adjacent (TOA)

determined without change or doubt
from the plan

$9^2 = ?$

Define demagogue:

81

a leader who gains power by appealing to emotions and prejudices

$10^2 = ?$

Define deride:

100

mock, ridicule, laugh at

$11^2 = ?$

Define despot:

121

to rule with oppression and tyranny

$12^2 = ?$

Define deter:

144

to prevent or discourage

$$1! = ?$$

Define digression:

1

a deviation or detour from the central
topic or focus

$2! = ?$

Define diligent:

2

persistent and hardworking

$3! = ?$

Define discredit:

6

to cause doubt or to harm the reputation of someone

$4! = ?$

Define disdain:

24

lack of respect or intense dislike

$$5! = ?$$

Define divergent:

120

to move apart in different directions

decimal of 1/8 = ?

Define elusive:

0.125

hard to find or catch

decimal of 3/8 = ?

Define empathy:

0.375

understanding of another's feelings

decimal of 5/8 = ?

Define emulate:

0.625

try to equal someone or something,
such as by imitating

decimal of 7/8 = ?

Define enhance:

0.875

to improve; increase clarity

$5*12 = ?$

Define enervating:

60

causing debilitation or weakness

$6*12 = ?$

Define ephemeral:

72

lasting only for a short period of time

$7*12 = ?$

Define evanescent:

84

disappearing after a short time and
quickly forgotten

$7*9 = ?$

Define exasperate:

63

worsen, make angry or frustrate

8*9 = ?

Define exemplary:

72

worthy of imitation, setting the example

14*5 = ?

Define extenuating:

70

diminish the seriousness of something

$14 * 6 = ?$

Define florid:

84

ornate in wording or style

$7*14 = ?$

Define forbearance:

98

a delay in enforcing legal right;
refraining from acting

8*14 = ?

Define fortitude:

112

strength and endurance during a difficult situation

$$9*14 = ?$$

Define fortuitous:

126

occurring by happy chance

$7*6 = ?$

Define foster:

42

providing parental care or to develop something

$7*7 = ?$

Define fraught:

49

filled with or accompanied by problems or difficulties

$7*8 = ?$

Define frugal:

56

avoiding waste, thrifty

$4*8 = ?$

Define gullible:

32

easily deceived or tricked

33*4 = ?

Define garble:

132

confuse, not understandable

33*5 = ?

Define hackneyed:

ordinary because of overuse

30*4 = ?

Define haughty:

120

acting arrogant or superior to others

24*6 = ?

Define hedonism:

144

seeking of selfish and sensual pleasures

18*3 = ?

Define hiatus:

54

a break, vacation from, or pause

19*3 = ?

Define hypothesis:

57

a theory that has not yet been tested or investigated

$17*3 = ?$

Define hyperbole:

51

exaggerating, making something more than it is

16*3 = ?

Define heresy:

48

against orthodox opinion or belief

$21*3 = ?$

Define impair:

63

to weaken or harm

22*4 = ?

Define impetuous:

88

undue haste without thought of consequences

72/8 = ?

Define impute:

9

to give credit of a usually undesirable action

$72/9 = ?$

Define imminent:

8

very likely going to happen

72/2 = ?

Define incompatible:

36

unable to be or work together

$68/4 = ?$

Define inconsequential:

17

something without importance or significance

68/2 = ?

Define inevitable:

34

impossible to avoid or prevent from happening

$64/4 = ?$

Define intrepid:

16

courageous and bold, without fear

64/8 = ?

Define integrity:

8

doing what is right, honest, or decent

58/2 = ?

Define intuitive:

29

to know by instinct alone

54/3 = ?

Define innocuous:

18

harmless

$48/4 = ?$

Define jubilation:

12

a feeling of extreme rejoicing and celebration

48/8 = ?

Define lobbyist:

6

someone who is paid to lobby, or persuade, political representatives, usually of a single particular issue.

$42/2 = ?$

Define longevity:

21

the property of having a long life

$36/12 = ?$

Define larceny:

3

theft, stealing

$120/4 = ?$

Define languid:

30

tired and slow

165/33 = ?

Define mundane:

5

common place, ordinary, or boring

104/13 = ?

Define nonchalant:

8

calm and unconcerned

96/12 = ?

Define novice:

8

a beginner, inexperienced

$108/9 = ?$

Define opulent:

12

rich and superior in quality

132/12 = ?

Define orator:

11

someone who delivers a speech or oration

$144/12 = ?$

Define ostentatious:

12

an intended and purposeful show of wealth intended to impress others

$65/5 = ?$

Define obsess:

13

always thinking about something constantly

78/6 = ?

Define paradox:

13

appearing conflicting or contradictory

$72/8 = ?$

Define parched:

9

lack of moisture and dried out by heat or sun

$70/5 = ?$

Define pragmatic:

14

concerned with practical matters and results

84/14 = ?

Define perfidious:

6

disloyal, not able to be trusted

$98/14 = ?$

Define precocious:

7

showing advanced development or
maturity at an early age

$112/8 = ?$

Define ponder:

14

think over, consider

$42/7 = ?$

Define pretentious:

6

acting more important or special than what is deserved

$49/7 = ?$

Define procrastinate:

7

to postpone doing something that needs to be done

$56/7 = ?$

Define prosaic:

8

lacking wit or imagination

32/8 = ?

Define prosperity:

4

the condition of being wealthy or successful

18+29 = ?

Define provocative:

47

purposefully exciting, arousing, or annoying someone

17+27 = ?

Define prudent:

44

careful and sensible; using good judgment

19+56 = ?

Define querulous:

75

always complaining or whining

25+42 = ?

Define rancorous:

67

having deeply held and long lasting resentment

22+35 = ?

Define reclusive:

57

withdrawn and alone from the world

37+28 = ?

Define reconciliation:

65

the end of conflict and reestablishing relationships or friendship

34+52 = ?

Define renovation:

86

repairing and restoring back to original or better state

35+17 = ?

Define restrained:

52

showing control and not giving into emotion or anger

18-56 = ?

Define respite:

-38

a break or intermission

25-42 = ?

Define resilient:

-17

quick to recover

22-45 = ?

Define reverence:

-23

a feeling of deep respect for someone or something

36-28 = ?

Define sagacity:

8

sound knowledge, judgment, and foresight

35-52 = ?

Define scrutinize:

-17

examine closely and carefully

$35 - 17 = ?$

Define spontaneous:

18

done with impulse and not as a result of planning

78-13 = ?

Define spurious:

65

something not genuine or authentic, as it might be claimed to be

67-25 = ?

Define submissive:

42

giving in to or following the authority
and demands of others

67-19 = ?

Define substantiate:

48

to confirm or prove something is true and valid

62-14 = ?

Define subtle:

48

understated and not obvious

63-19 = ?

Define superficial:

44

shallow in character and attitude, only concerned with things on the surface

57-19 = ?

Define superfluous:

38

more than is needed, desired, or necessary

In a class of 42 students, 18 are boys. Two girls get transferred to another school. What percent of students remaining are girls?
  a) 14%.
  b) 16%.
  c) 52.4%.
  d) 60%.
  e) None of the above.

Define terse:

Answer: e)
The entire class has 42 students, 18 of which are boys, meaning 42 - 18 = 24 is the number of girls. Out of these 24 girls, 2 leave; so 22 girls are left. The total number of students is now 42 - 2 = 40.
22/40 * 100 = 55%.

Reminder: If you forget to subtract 2 from the total number of students, you will end up with 60% as the answer. Sometimes you may calculate an answer that has been given as a choice; it can still be incorrect. Always check your answer.

to the point, concise

A sweater goes on sale for 30% off. If the original price was $70, what is the discounted price?
   a) $48.
   b) $49.
   c) $51.
   d) $65.
   e) $52.

Define transient:

Answer: b)
New price = original price * (1 − discount) →
new price = 70(1-.3) = 49.

lasting for only a short time or duration

If test A is taken 5 times with an average result of 21, and test B is taken 13 times with an average result of 23, what is the combined average?
   a) 22.24.
   b) 22.22.
   c) 22.00.
   d) 22.44.
   e) 24.22.

Define trite:

Answer : d)
If test A avg = 21 for 5 tests, then sum of test A results = 21 * 5 = 105.
If test B avg = 23 for 13 tests, then sum of test B results = 23 * 13 = 299.
So total result = 299 + 105 = 404.
Average of all tests = 404/(5 + 13) = 404/18 = 22.44.

dull, common

A set of data has 12 entries. The average of the first 6 entries is 12, the average of the next two entries is 20, and the average of the remaining entries is 4. What is the average of the entire data set?
 a) 10.
 b) 10.67.
 c) 11.
 d) 12.67.
 e) 10.5.

Define timorous:

Answer: b)
- The average of the first 6 points is 12 → $s_1/6 = 12$ → $s_1 = 72$; s_1 is the sum of the first 6 points.
- The average of the next 2 points is 20 → $s_2/2 = 20$ → $s_2 = 40$; s_2 is the sum of the next 2 points.
- The average of the remaining 4 points is 4 → $s_3/4 = 4$ → $s_3 = 16$; s_3 is the sum of the last 4 points.
- The sum of all the data points = 72 + 40 + 16 = 128. The average = 128/12 = 10.67.

cowardly, fearful

What is $x^2y^3z^5/y^2z^{-9}$?
 a) y^5z^4.
 b) yz^4.
 c) x^2yz^{14}.
 d) $x^2y^5z^4$.
 e) xyz.

Define thwart:

Answer: **c)**
$x^2y^3z^5/y^2z^{-9} = x^2y^3z^5 * y^{-2}z^9$ which gives the answer $x^2y^{(3-2)}z^{(5+9)}$ → x^2yz^{14}.

to prevent or frustrate

What is k if $(2m^3)^5 = 32m^{k+1}$?
 a) 11.
 b) 12.
 c) 13.
 d) 14.
 e) 15.

Define venerable:

Answer: d)
Expand $(2m^3)^5$ to give $32m^{15}$.

So $32m^{15} = 32m^{k+1}$ → $k+1 = 15$ → $k = 14$.

worthy of respect because of wisdom or age

The number 568cd should be divisible by 2, 5, and 7. What are the values of the digits c and d?
   a) 56835.
   b) 56830.
   c) 56860.
   d) 56840.
   e) 56800.

Define vindicate:

Answer: d)
If the number is divisible by 2, d should be even. If the number is divisible by 5, then b has to equal 0.

Start by making both variables 0 and dividing by the largest factor, 7. $56800/7 = 8114$.

2 from 56800 is 56798, a number divisible by 2 and 7.

Next add a multiple of 7 that turns the last number to a 0. $6 * 7 = 42$. $56798 + 42 = 56840$, which is divisible by 2, 5, and 7.

proving someone or something
innocent and free of blame or guilt

Carla is 3 times older than her sister Megan. Eight years ago, Carla was 18 years older than her sister. What is Megan's age?
    a) 10.
    b) 8.
    c) 9.
    d) 6.
    e) 5.

Define venerate:

Answer: c)
Carla's age is c; Megan's age is m. $c = 3m$; $c - 8 = m - 8 + 18$.

Substitute $3m$ for c in equation 2 → $3m - 8 = m + 10$ → $m = 9$.

to regard with much respect

If $x < 5$ and $y < 6$, then $x + y$ __?__ 11.
   a) $<$
   b) $>$
   c) $\leq$
   d) $\geq$
   e) $=$

Define wary:

Answer: a)
Choice **a)** will always be true, while the other choices can never be true.

Answer: b)
$25x^2 - 40x + 32 < 22 \rightarrow 25x^2 - 40x + 16 < 6 \rightarrow (5x - 4)^2 < 6 \rightarrow 5x - 4 < 6$.

$x = 2$, so x has to be all numbers less than 2 for this inequality to work.

to be cautious or suspicious

Which of the following is true about the inequality
$25x^2 - 40x - 32 < 22$?
  a) There are no solutions.
  b) There is a set of solutions.
  c) There is 1 solution only.
  d) There are 2 solutions.
  e) There are 3 solutions.

Define abut:

Answer: b)
$25x^2 - 40x + 32 < 22$ → $25x^2 - 40x + 16 < 6$ → $(5x - 4)^2 < 6$ → $5x - 4 < 6$.

$x = 2$, so x has to be all numbers less than 2 for this inequality to work.

To touch at the end or boundaries

What is the equation of the line that passes through (3, 5), with intercept $y = 8$?
   a) $y = x + 8$.
   b) $y = x - 8$.
   c) $y = -x - 8$.
   d) $y = -x + 8$.
   e) $y = -x$.

Define acquiesce:

Answer: d)

The standard form of the line equation is $y = mx + b$. We need to find slope m.

$m = (y_2 - y_1)/(x_2 - x_1)$ → $m = (5 - 8)/(3 - 0)$ → $m = -1$.

Therefore the equation is $y = -x + 8$.

To Comply or submit

What is the value of y in the equation $(3x - 4)^2 = 4y - 15$, if $x = 3$?
   a) 10.
   b) 2.5.
   c) -10.
   d) -2.5.
   e) 5.

Define amateur:

Answer: a)
At $x = 3$, $((3*3) - 4)^2 = 4y - 15$.

$(9 - 4)^2 = 4y - 15$.

$25 = 4y - 15$.

$40 = 4y$.

$y = 10$.

Practicing an art or occupation for the love of it, but not as a profession.

Factor $x^2 + 2x - 15$.
   a) $(x - 3)(x + 5)$.
   b) $(x + 3)(x - 5)$.
   c) $(x + 3)(x + 5)$.
   d) $(x - 3)(x - 5)$.
   e) $(x - 1)(x + 15)$.

Define Ameliorate:

Answer: **a)**
The constant term is -15. The factors should multiply to give -15 and add to give 2.
The numbers -3 and 5 satisfy both, $(x - 3)(x + 5)$.

To relieve, as from pain or hardship

Car A starts at 3:15 PM and travels straight to its destination at a constant speed of 50 mph. If it arrives at 4:45 PM, how far did it travel?
 a) 70 miles.
 b) 75 miles.
 c) 65 miles.
 d) 40 miles.
 e) 105 miles.

Define baffle:

Answer: b)
The time between 3:15 PM and 4:45 PM = 1.5 hours. 1.5 * 50 = 75.

Reminder: half an hour is written as .5 of an hour, not .3 of an hour, even though on a clock a half hour is 30 minutes.

To foil or frustrate.

What is the area, in square feet, of the triangle whose sides have lengths equal to 3, 4, and 5 feet?

- a) 6 square feet.
- b) 7 square feet.
- c) 4 square feet.
- d) 5 square feet.
- e) 8 square feet.

Define benevolence:

Answer: a)
The Pythagorean triple (special right triangle property) means the two shorter sides form a right triangle.

$1/2 bh = A$. So, $(1/2)(3)(4) = 6$.

Any act of kindness or well-doing

In the following figure, where AE bisects line BC, and angles AEC and AEB are both right angles, what is the length of AB?

a) 1 cm.
b) 2 cm.
c) 3 cm.
d) 4 cm.
e) 5 cm.

BC = 6 cm
AD = 3 cm
CD = 4 cm

Define blemish:

Answer: e)
$AB^2 = AC^2 = AD2 + CD^2 \rightarrow AB^2 = 3^2 + 4^2 \rightarrow AB = 5$.

A mark that mars beauty.

The wardrobe of a studio contains 4 hats, 3 suits, 5 shirts, 2 pants, and 3 pairs of shoes. How many different ways can these items be put together?
 a) 60.
 b) 300.
 c) 360.
 d) 420.
 e) 500.

Define botany:

Answer: c)
The number of ways = 4 * 3 * 5 * 2 * 3 = 360.

The science that treats of plants.

For lunch, you have a choice between chicken fingers or cheese sticks for an appetizer; turkey, chicken, or veal for the main course; cake or pudding for dessert; and either Coke or Pepsi for a beverage. How many choices of possible meals do you have?
   a) 16.
   b) 24.
   c) 34.
   d) 36.
   e) 8.

Define Braggart:

Answer: b)
Multiply the possible number of choices for each item from which you can choose.

2 * 3 * 2 * 2 = 24.

A vain boaster.

A class has 50% more boys than girls. What is the ratio of boys to girls?
   a) 4:3.
   b) 3:2.
   c) 5:4.
   d) 10:7.
   e) 7:5.

Define Cajole:

Answer: b)
The ratio of boys to girls is 150:100, or 3:2.

To impose on or dupe by flattering speech.

A car can travel 30 miles on 4 gallons of gas. If the gas tank has a capacity of 16 gallons, how far can it travel if the tank is ¾ full?
    a) 120 miles.
    b) 90 miles.
    c) 60 miles.
    d) 55 miles.
    e) 65 miles.

Define Candor:

Answer: b)
A full tank has 16 gallons → 3/4 of the tank = 12 gallons. The car can travel 30 miles on 4 gallons, so 12 gallons would take the car 12 * 30/4 = 90 miles.

The quality of frankness or outspokenness.

What is the value of $f(x) = (x^2 - 25)/(x + 5)$ when $x = 0$?
   a) -1.
   b) -2.
   c) -3.
   d) -4.
   e) -5.

Define Capitulate:

Answer: e)
We know $(x^2 - 25) = (x + 5)(x - 5)$.

So $(x^2 - 25)/(x + 5) = x - 5$. At $x = 0, f(0) = -5$.

To surrender or stipulate terms.

Four years from now, John will be twice as old as Sally will be. If Sally was 10 eight years ago, how old is John?
    a) 35.
    b) 40.
    c) 45.
    d) 50.
    e) 55.

Define Castigate:

Answer: b)
Let j be John's age and s be Sally's age.

$j + 4 = 2(s + 4)$.

$s - 8 = 10$ ➔ $s = 18$.

So $j + 4 = 2(18 + 4)$ ➔ $j = 40$.

To punish